THE BRIDE OF CHRIST

For Judy,
Thank you for
taking care of my
grandmother. I hope this
study is a blessing!
Rachel Nanco

The

BRIDE

OF

CHRIST

RACHEL MEEKS

ISBN 978-1-944704-39-1

Published by Start2Finish
Fort Worth, Texas 76244
www.start2finish.org

Printed in the United States of America

Unless otherwise noted, all Scripture quotations are from The Holy Bible, English Standard Version®, copyright © 2001 by Crossway Bibles, a publishing ministry of Good News Publishers. Used by permission. All rights reserved.

Cover Design: Evangela Creative

For Ross, the man who made me a bride.

CONTENTS

Wives, submit to your own husbands, as to the Lord. For the husband is the head of the wife even as Christ is the head of the church, his body, and is himself its Savior. Now as the church submits to Christ, so also wives should submit in everything to their husbands. Husbands, love your wives, as Christ loved the church and gave himself up for her, that he might sanctify her, having cleansed her by the washing of water with the word, so that he might present the church to himself in splendor, without spot or wrinkle or any such thing, that she might be holy and without blemish. In the same way husbands should love their wives as their own bodies. He who loves his wife loves himself. For no one ever hated his own flesh, but nourishes and cherishes it, just as Christ does the church, because we are members of his body. "Therefore a man shall leave his father and mother and hold fast to his wife, and the two shall become one flesh." This mystery is profound, and I am saying that it refers to Christ and the church.

Ephesians 5:22-32

INTRODUCTION

$\mathcal{J}$ stood arm-in with my father as the church doors opened. Everyone I knew and loved rose to their feet to watch me walk down the aisle. I remember having a hard time catching my breath at being the center of attention for over two hundred people. Next to the man who baptized me, stood my soon-to-be husband grinning like the luckiest man alive. And, for some reason, he believed he was.

We said our vows, exchanged rings, and signed our marriage certificate. We laughed and enjoyed the company of our friends and family. Then we left and went to our new home and, later on, to a bed and breakfast in Asheville, North Carolina. In which part of that day did we join our lives together? Was it the vows? The piece of paper we signed and turned in to the probate office? Sleeping together? If one part was left out, would we still be married?

In Ephesians 5:30, we read, "For we are members of His body, of His flesh and of His bones." The latter half of Ephesians is the center of many, presumably most, classes, sermons, and books regarding marriage. Wives submit, husbands love—we know the drill. Or do we?

> Husbands, love your wives, as Christ loved the church
> and gave himself up for her, that he might sanctify
> her, having cleansed her by the washing of water with
> the word, so that he might present the church to himself in splendor, without spot or wrinkle or any such
> thing, that she might be holy and without blemish.
> Ephesians 5:25-27

Jesus here, and in many other Scriptures, is described as the husband of the Church. As part of the Church, we are part of the Bride of Christ. However, we are unfamiliar with what marriage meant to the first century Christians reading Ephesians. We need to lay aside our preconceived notions about weddings, bride prices, and divorce and look at this with fresh eyes so we can appreciate how God views us as His chosen people.

If you ever wondered why God made mankind with all its problems and strife, I would ask you why do people marry? Even the most captivated bride and groom know that they will have problems and that a large percentage of marriages end in divorce. However, people still flock to the altar because of the hope of love, relationship, and intimacy. God wants the same thing every groom wants as he watches his bride walk down the aisle. He wants to love a pure and faithful entity and be loved in return.

1

THE FIRST WEDDING

In the beginning God created the heavens and the earth—and marriage. As you read Genesis 1, notice that everything comes in pairs: the heavens and the earth, day and night, waters over water. The creation of vegetation is the first hint of reproduction, which obviously requires more than one being. The sun and moon are coupled as a greater light to rule the day and a lesser light to rule the night. Fish, birds, animals all come as male and female. Even later, in Genesis 2, we see the creation of two trees: the tree of the knowledge of good and evil and the tree of life. All these pairs have a connection with each other and with their Creator. The natural laws God put in place define the association between the sun and the moon, the atmosphere and the seas. Living creatures procreate and have varying and complex relationships with each other based on their instincts. It is what we call nature, but for mankind, some things are different, which is fitting because only mankind is made in God's image and has received His breath of life.

> Then God said, "Let us make man in our image, after our likeness. And let them have dominion over the fish of the sea and over the birds of the heavens and over the livestock and over all the earth and over every creeping thing that creeps on the earth." So God created man in his own image, in the image of God he created him; male and female he created them.
>
> Genesis 1:26-27

Both male and female are made in the image of God. Only together, not apart, do we see the whole character of God in human form. Therefore, when we move on to the second chapter in Genesis and learn that God made Adam out of the ground, we realize that Adam, by himself, was incomplete. He was the only creation made without his complement. We read that God gave Adam a home, the beautiful garden of Eden. He gave him work and purpose in tending the garden. God also gave Adam his one moral boundary. Only then did God remark, "It is not good that the man should be alone; I will make him a helper fit for him." Then, God parades all the beasts of the field and birds of the air before Adam seeing what he will call them. And, obviously, Adam saw that all these animals were designed biologically to have mates, as was he, in fact. Yet, "for Adam there was not found a helper fit for him."

What was God's purpose in delaying the creation of woman?

Now, for the romantic part. God put Adam to sleep and took from him a rib and formed woman from it and "brought her to the man." We typically suffer from the idea of God being a hovering spirit or something to that effect, but remember, mankind was made in the image of God; therefore, in some way, we look like God. In Genesis Chapter 3, we read about God walking in the garden, as in God had to have legs and a body like us. So, when we read that God brought her to Adam, he didn't just drop her off and look down on them from a cloud. The wording implies that God walked up with Woman and put her hand in Adam's. And Adam, fresh from naming all of creation turns to God and says,

> Then the man said, "This at last is bone of my bones and flesh of my flesh; she shall be called Woman, because she was taken out of Man."
>
> Genesis 2:23

The Bible goes on to narrate in verses 24-25, "Therefore a man shall leave his father and his mother and hold fast to his wife, and they shall become one flesh. And the man and his wife were both naked and were not ashamed." We are reading about the first wedding! Notice the bride's Creator (or Father) brought her to her intended and gave her to him. The man claims her and gives her his name. The Hebrew word translated in verse 24 as "hold fast" can also be translated as "cleave" or "joined together."

Read this commentary on head-coverings and then read 1

Corinthians 11:2-16:

Roman statuary depicts emperors and senior magistrates as partially covering their heads with folds of their togas when offering a public sacrifice ("praying") or reading its entrails ("prophesying"). Paul instructs the Corinthian men not to dishonor Christ by praying to Him in the same way that others addressed false gods such as Apollo. By praying with their heads uncovered, they show they are praying in a new way and worshiping a different deity than their pagan neighbors. Women were to cover their heads because, in the first century, a woman with uncovered hair was signaling that she was single or sexually available, thereby shaming her husband. The symbol of authority on her head (v. 10) was the covering indicating a woman's marital status. Women were encouraged to prophesy or pray without bringing shame onto the assembly. In Greco-Roman culture, long hair (v.14) on a man was the hairstyle of a juvenile or barbarian; it signified an effeminate, weak man, easily conquered. Paul desires men to look like men and women to look like women, each sex respecting its created identity and role in both appearance and action.[1]

> **According to 1 Corinthians 11:7-12. Why is it important that man was created before woman?**

_____

_____

1.   *Crossway Archeology Bible*, pg. 1710.

Generations pass, but God's design for mankind to dwell joined with one another remains. Traditions and customs develop that define marriage. To understand them, I invite you to imagine you are a young Hebrew girl.

You have bled and are considered a woman now, ready for marriage. You learn to spin and weave from your mother. You help the servants cook and thresh grain. The farthest you wander from your house is the well outside the gates where you draw water every morning and evening. This evening is like any other. The air is cooling quickly as you walk with the water jar on your shoulder. Many other girls are gathered at the well, as always, and you wait your turn to draw. You dip your jar into the well, fill it to the brim, and turn for home. Your attention is drawn to a man running towards you from a group of servants tending a train of camels.

"Please give me a little water to drink from your jar," he pleads. The man is older and well dressed in rich fabric, though dirty from what appears to be a very long journey.

"Drink, my lord," you reply and quickly let down your jar from your shoulder, so he can drink. As he drinks, you notice that the camels are pulling at their tethers to come near the well. They smell the water and evidently have not yet been given the chance to drink. You have been taught from the time you were a small child that hospitality is the foremost courtesy, so as soon as the man finishes drinking, you offer to water his camels. You empty your jar in the trough by the camels and begin drawing jar after jar of water. Finally, the camels pick up their heads satisfied, and you turn to fill the jar once more with water to take home. Before you can, however, the man takes your hand and gently slides a beautiful bracelet over your wrist. He takes the other hand and places another heavy band on your arm and places a golden ring in your nose.

You look up at him in astonishment at these costly gifts, and he asks you, "Please tell me whose daughter you are. Is there room in your father's house for us to spend the night?"

You look at the dozen or so men with him and smile as you answer proudly, "I am the daughter of Bethuel, the son of Milcah, whom she bore to Nahor."

The man's wrinkled face breaks into a huge smile as he squeezes your hand.

"We have plenty of both straw and fodder and room to spend the night," you add.

The man then releases you and bows in worship, saying, "Blessed be Yahweh, the God of my master Abraham, who has not forsaken his steadfast love and his faithfulness toward my master. As for me, the Lord has led me in the way to the house of my master's kinsmen."

If you were this young Hebrew girl, then your name would be Rebekah, and you would be about to get married. The account is found in Genesis 24. Abraham's servant lays his whole case before Rebekah's family, and her father and brother agree for Rebekah to be Isaac's wife. The servant gives costly gifts to both Rebekah and her family, and she is asked if she will begin the long journey to her husband the very next day, to which she agrees. Her family gives her several servant girls, including the servant that has taken care of her from the time of her infancy, and they depart.

> **We all grow up with legends. The stories we hear as a child shape our beliefs, morals, and ambitions. Why did Abraham want a bride taken for his son from his own family? And why do you think Rebekah went with the servant so willingly?**

Put yourself in her shoes again for the romantic part.

After many days, you see the land to which you now belong. The fields are rich with grain, and wooded hills can be seen in the distance. The sun is getting low on your right, but the servant has assured you that they should be able to make it to his master's dwelling before nightfall. You lift your eyes to a rise in the fields and see a man walking towards the caravan. Your stomach flutters as you are helped down from your camel. "Who is that man walking towards us?" you ask.

"It is my master," the servant replies.

You quickly veil yourself with one of the beautiful fabrics that were gifted to you by this man who you will meet as a husband.

The servant stops the train and tells you to wait while he walks ahead to speak with his master. Though the light is fading, you watch in earnest to catch a glimpse of your husband. Eliezer has told you that he is a man in his prime and will inherit everything his father owns—which is considerable. His mother died not long ago, and he has taken the death very hard. Eliezer reports that he is a good man, like his father, who seeks to please the Lord.

Your heart beats furiously as servant and master turn to come to you. "Will I please him?" you wonder. "What if I am not who the Lord intended?"

In the fading light, you see that your husband is a handsome man with steady features. He reaches out for your hand, which you give him. He leads you through the fields and tells you that his tent is not far. Your hand trembles slightly within his, but he squeezes it gently to reassure you. His voice is low and calming as he tells you things about the land and how beautiful the woodlands are to the west. His tent comes into view, and you know you are home.

Then Isaac brought her into the tent of Sarah his mother and took Rebekah, and she became his wife, and he loved her. So Isaac was comforted after his mother's death.

Genesis 24:67

Which part of the story made Isaac and Rebekah man and wife?

_____

_____

_____

Part of what makes the Bible amazing is its brevity. The Spirit of God only included what we need to know. Moses was also writing to an audience that was practicing the same social norms as Isaac and Rebekah. We, thousands of years later and on the other side of the world, have different traditions that define what it looks like to get married. If I were to tell you that my wedding took place in a church, that we had five groomsmen and five bridesmaids, and that we lit a unity candle, you would have an idea of what my wedding looked like. I wouldn't have to tell you it was officiated by a preacher, we had a reception, or that we signed a marriage license. You would assume those things because that is what weddings of our day look like. I believe that Moses includes the distinguishing things about

Rebekah and Isaac's marriage and doesn't include what would be obvious to the Israelites. Moses includes how God directs the servant to Rebekah, that costly gifts were given to Rebekah and her family, and that Rebekah came to Isaac immediately. These are the extraordinary things about the marriage.

With godly wisdom, Abraham knew a woman from his family would have grown up hearing how God spoke to him, calling him away from his family into an unknown land. She should have heard how much God has blessed him since that time, and the rich gifts he sends would prove it. This bride's faith in the Lord would have already been planted, and she could be counted on not to lure Isaac away with other gods.

> **What does Abraham and his servant teach us about finding a spouse whether for ourselves or our children? Read 2 Corinthians 6:14-18.**

_____

_____

_____

Abraham's family will grow. There will be brides married and sons born. However, just as in the garden, the temptation to leave the God that created them and set them apart will always be there. Just as Rebekah, you and I were called before the foundations of the world to be a part of God's holy people. However, you came to know the truth, trust that God guided that path from person to person all the way back to a simple carpenter's son in Galilee. He has great plans for you as part of His family.

MARRIAGE

he story of Jacob's marriages, even with all their dysfunction, gives us a great example of how the people of the ancient Near East got married. Using this story, we will break down the three-step process ingrained in God's people as their way of becoming married. Covenant, Consummation, and Celebration. But first, read Genesis 29 before continuing.

COVENANT

When Laban asks Jacob what wages he wanted, Jacob responds that he wants to marry his daughter, Rachel, in lieu of wages. Traditionally, a bride price was given for a woman. The bride price would vary in each region, but whatever it was, Jacob valued it at seven years of labor. That is a valuable bride. For a couple to be considered married, the groom or the groom's father (or servant in Isaac and Rebekah's case) would first sit down with the bride's father and establish a covenant, or contractual agreement. The bride price would be set as well as the time before the couple could cohabitate. Other terms could be added as well, such as the groom agreeing to not take any more wives and providing his wife with her due of clothes, food, and sex (Read Exodus 21:10 if you think I'm kidding. A woman needed her husband to sleep with her so she would have a son whose duty was to care for her in her old age). Once the covenant was agreed upon and the bride price paid, the couple was considered married. Notice in Genesis 29:21, Jacob calls Rachel his wife before they had cohabitated.

> The Hebrew word for "covenant" means "solemn promise or agreement," but it most literally means "cutting," as in "cutting off a choice piece of meat for yourself" or "cutting animals in two." In Genesis 15, Abram was arranging a covenant ratification ritual typical of ancient Near Eastern covenant agreements. The purpose was to invoke a curse; those who violated the covenant would face the same fate as the slain animals."[1] What does this say about marriage? Read Mark 10:7-9.

_____

_____

_____

1.   *ESV Archeology Bible.* pg. 36.

The purpose of the bride price and dowry (land or money given to the bride by her father) is to give the bride means to set up her house and to give her something to live on in the event of her husband's death or divorce. The reason the bride price is given to the father is that men took care of matters of business and because he would stand as a witness that the money went to his daughter. It is within the father's right to take some of the bride price. After all, he is losing an active contributor to the economy of his house. All girls would weave, care for sheep, help bring in the crop, etc. That said, most of the bride price is expected to go to the bride. Wealthy fathers were also expected to give their daughters a dowry and at least one handmaid when it's time for her to go to her husband's house. The handmaid would be a slave girl whose job was to be the daughter's chief servant and to be a concubine in the event the bride is barren.

> **In Genesis 31, Jacob decides to flee from Laban, but before he does, he talks to his wives. What do we learn about their bride prices from their conversation in Genesis 31:14-16?**

_____

_____

_____

In Genesis 31, we read about the confrontation between Jacob and Laban after Jacob fled with his wives, children, and flocks. This account records the first verbal marriage covenant in the Bible. Traditionally, this would have been established first, but it seems that when the marriage agreement was first reached, Jacob and Laban thought that Jacob would be staying with him indefinitely, so the particulars weren't hammered out. Laban begins in verse 44, "Now therefore, come, let us make a covenant, you and I, and let it be a witness between you and me." Laban continues in verse 49, "May the LORD watch between you and me when we are absent one from another. If you afflict my daughters, or if you take other wives besides my daughters, although no man is with us—see, God is witness between you and me!"

Jacob and Laban swore oaths and set up a pillar as a witness between them. They make sacrifices to the Lord and eat together as is common upon the establishment of a covenant. Later, written marriage covenants become commonplace, and many have been found throughout the Middle East.

> **Can you think of a strange price set on a bride? Check out 1 Samuel 18:25 and Joshua15:16-17. How does the bride price affect the quality of the husband?**

_____

_____

_____

CONSUMMATION

Jacob was no poet as we read in Genesis 29:21, "Give me my wife, for my days are fulfilled, that I may go in to her." The covenant set a price as well as a time before the couple can live together. Normally, the time between the establishment of the covenant and cohabitation was to give time for the groom to prepare a house for his wife, but here we see an unusual setup with the groom being a member of the father's household. Either way, after seven years, it's time to get down to business.

The bride would be bathed and dressed in fine clothes and jewels. She would be veiled as well. The groom would come to her father's house dressed in his finest and lead her to his home. This procession normally happened at evening and was considered the most important part of the ceremony. This was the transferring of the bride's welfare from the father to the bridegroom in the presence of witnesses.

> In Matthew 25:1-13, we read the parable of the ten virgins. These women would have been the bride's companions or servants and would be part of this important wedding procession. Think of the anticipation and preparation that goes into a wedding, yet the five foolish virgins were not ready for this place of honor that was appointed for them. How does this parable relate to us?

_____

_____

_____

Once in the husband's home, vows would be said, and the

couple would be blessed before being escorted to their room where the couple would consummate their marriage. Pretty standard except there would be witnesses in the morning wanting to check the sheets to make sure the bride was a virgin. You see, lineage was everything. If a bride was not a virgin, the groom could not be sure that the children she bore were his. The first son would be his heir and the one to carry on his name. There can be no room for error. Check out Deuteronomy 22:13-21. This custom is strange to us, but the blood was evidence of the bride's purity. Women were extremely vulnerable in this culture, and God's laws shielded them from mistreatment.

> **It's hard for us to understand the reality for women of Bible times. The repercussions for a woman being raped (Exodus 22:16-17; Deuteronomy 22:28-29) confuses and troubles many. Why should a woman marry her rapist? Is it better for the woman if she doesn't (e.g., 2 Samuel 13:11-20)?**

_____

_____

_____

Anyways, back to Jacob and Rachel—I mean, Leah. Yes, Jacob wakes to find he married the wrong sister. Laban tricked him into working for him another seven years and has married off two daughters without having to give them their bride price. (On a side note: my theory around Leah's "weak eyes" is that she had poor eyesight. That would obviously detract from her value as a wife). Modern Jewish weddings have actually incorporated an "unveiling" where the bride appears to the groom before the wedding, unveiled for the groom to ensure that she is his chosen bride. He then veils her for the wedding.

> **Why didn't Jacob just return Leah and demand for Rachel? How does this deception change the dynamics of Jacob's family (And I'm not talking about the problems that come with polygamy)?**

_____

_____

_____

CELEBRATION

Laban tells Jacob to give Leah her "week." This is referring to the traditional seven-day feast to celebrate the wedding. This feast is held at the groom's house to celebrate the arrival of the bride, while another seven-day feast is held when the covenant is first made at the bride's father's house. This was not just a polite dinner, but an important part of the marriage. This celebration, along with the celebration at the creation of the covenant agreement, did three things. 1) It provided witnesses that the betrothal and marriage have taken place. If the wife or husband was going to take their spouse to court at some point, they would first need witnesses to prove they were married. 2) In this culture, hospitality was very important. To take someone into your house means they are under your protection. Which means violence cannot take place between you. This was a society where war and feuds were common. Covenants always include a feast to cement peace (Genesis 26:28-31). 3) Feasts are fun, and a marriage was a cause to celebrate.

> In Matthew 22:1-14, we read the parable of the wedding feast. The invitation to the feast went first to the Jews as God's chosen people, but they rejected Jesus and even killed the prophets that came to tell them about the coming bridegroom. Therefore, God (the king) invited all who would listen, both good and bad. However, at the feast, the king noticed that someone was not wearing their "wedding garment," so the king cast him out into outer darkness. We assume that wedding garments were at the least one's best set of clean clothes, but they could have been robes that were gifted to them by the king for the wedding. Why was the king so offended? How does the parable apply to us as members of the kingdom of God?

_____

_____

_____

GOD'S FIRST WIFE

You will lead the people You have redeemed with Your faithful love; You will guide them to Your holy dwelling with Your strength.

Exodus 15:13 HCSB

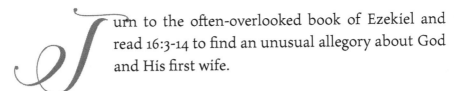urn to the often-overlooked book of Ezekiel and read 16:3-14 to find an unusual allegory about God and His first wife.

How does this allegory change the way you view God's relationship with Israel? Does it change the way you view your own relationship with God?

COVENANT

> I made my vow to you and entered into a covenant with you, declares the Lord GOD, and you became mine.
>
> Ezekiel 16:8b

When did God make His vow to the nation of Israel?

> Now the LORD said to Abram, "Go from your country and your kindred and your father's house to the land that I will show you. And I will make of you a great nation, and I will bless you and make your name great, so that you will be a blessing. I will bless those who bless you, and him who dishonors you I will curse, and in you all the families of the earth shall be blessed."
>
> Genesis 12:1-3

The Lord calls Abram from his father's house, just as Eliezer called Rebekah. Abram acts in faith and obeys the Lord, never seeing his family again. However, years pass without the fulfillment of God's promises. Abram is despairing because though the Lord has promised a great nation through him, he remains childless.

> "Fear not, Abram, I am your shield; your reward shall be very great." But Abram said, "O Lord GOD, what will you give me, for I continue childless, and the heir of my house is Eliezer of Damascus?" And Abram said, "Behold, you have given me no offspring, and a member of my household will be my heir." And behold, the word of the LORD came to him: "This

man shall not be your heir; your very own son shall be your heir." And he brought him outside and said, "Look toward heaven, and number the stars, if you are able to number them." Then he said to him, "So shall your offspring be." And he believed the LORD, and he counted it to him as righteousness. [...] On that day the LORD made a covenant with Abram, saying, "To your offspring I give this land, from the river of Egypt to the great river, the river Euphrates."

Genesis 15:1b-6, 18

> **We studied the significance of the sacrifices God instructed Abram to make in the last chapter. This is a binding covenant made by God, yet in the very next chapter, we read about Sarai offering Hagar, her servant, to Abram as a concubine. Check it out in Genesis 16. The account of Sarai and Hagar is a perfect example of what happens when we believe that God needs us for His will to be fulfilled. As brides of Christ, what can we learn from this story?**

In every culture, a social norm develops so that men can distinguish between single and married women. Brides take their husband's name. They wear wedding rings. In other cultures, women wear their hair up or in braids. Some wear face paint. In Jewish culture and many others, married women covered their hair. God also required His people to show a mark of the covenant between them.

> When Abram was ninety-nine years old the LORD appeared to Abram and said to him, "I am God Almighty; walk before me, and be blameless, that I may make my covenant between me and you, and may multiply you greatly." Then Abram fell on his face. And God said to him, "Behold, my covenant is with you, and you shall be the father of a multitude of nations. No longer shall your name be called Abram, but your name shall be Abraham, for I have made you the father of a multitude of nations. [...] And God said to Abraham, "As for you, you shall keep my covenant, you and your offspring after you throughout their generations. This is my covenant, which you shall keep, between me and you and your offspring after you: Every male among you shall be circumcised. You shall be circumcised in the flesh of your foreskins, and it shall be a sign of the covenant between me and you. [...] Any uncircumcised male who is not circumcised in the flesh of his foreskin shall be cut off from his people; he has broken my covenant."
>
> Genesis 17:1-5, 9-11, 14

In Exodus 4:24-26, we read a very strange account where the Lord almost killed Moses on his way to Egypt. Why did the Lord do this?

God renamed Sarai as well as Abram since she and Abram together made the unit through which the promised child could come. In the garden, God created them male and female because only together do they represent the character of God. God is essentially marrying Abram and Sarai. He gives them great wealth, makes a covenant with them, changes their names, and requires them to circumcise all males to show that they are bound to God.

> **Study the language God uses in Genesis 17:15-21. What do these verses signify?**

_____

_____

_____

CONSUMMATION

Then I bathed you with water and washed off your blood from you and anointed you with oil.

Ezekiel 16:9

If a bridegroom was coming from a long way off to claim his bride, she would prepare a room in her father's house to receive him before they journeyed back to his home. The bride would ceremonially cleanse herself by immersing in water. She would anoint herself with fragrant oil and wear her finest clothes. Great care would be given in the cleansing and decorating of this room, as well, because this was where the bride and bridegroom would consummate their marriage.

God made His covenant with Abraham. And Abraham and all his male descendants were circumcised to show their commitment to God. While in Egypt, Abraham's children, the Israelites, wait for the Lord to take them to the land that was promised, just as a bride waits for her husband to take her to his home. Over four hundred years pass before a shepherd stops to look at a bush that was not consumed even though it was on fire.

God leads his people out of bondage with great wonders through His servant Moses. He then takes them to the wilderness, where he instructs Moses to build a tabernacle so the Lord can dwell with His people. Intricate detail is given on how to build the Tabernacle. Twelve chapters of Exodus are devoted to it. The Lord puts His Spirit on Oholiab and Bezalel to give them the skill and intelligence needed to construct the Tabernacle. The curtains are woven in the finest blue, purple, and scarlet thread. All the articles inside the Tabernacle are made of gold. The altar and laver outside are made of bronze. The High Priest's garments are made of the finest woven linen. A golden ephod inlaid with jewels is worn on his chest. A golden band is fitted on his forehead that reads "HOLINESS TO THE LORD."

> Then the cloud covered the tent of meeting, and the glory of the LORD filled the tabernacle. [...] For the cloud of the LORD was on the tabernacle by day, and fire was in it by night, in the sight of all the house of Israel throughout all their journeys.
>
> Exodus 40:34, 38

The Tabernacle was also always placed in the center of camp, and when they reached Canaan, it was set up in the middle of the country, so God could always be the midst of His people. But what was required for the people to be able to be in the presence of God? Blood.

> **How is blood connected with purity?**

_____

_____

Before the construction of the Tabernacle in Exodus 24, Moses and the nation of Israel stand before the thundering mountain of God. Moses sets up twelve pillars representing the twelve tribes and sacrifices oxen to the Lord.

> And Moses took half of the blood and put it in basins, and half of the blood he threw against the altar. Then he took the Book of the Covenant and read it in the hearing of the people. And they said, "All that the LORD has spoken we will do, and we will be obedient." And Moses took the blood and threw it on the people and said, "Behold the blood of the covenant that the LORD has made with you in accordance with all these words."
> Exodus 24:6-8

The reason that the father of a Hebrew bride kept the cloth that she lay on when her marriage was consummated was because the blood represented her innocence. The blood that Moses sprinkles on the Israelites purified them, allowing them to be in the presence of God. The blood of countless animals continually purified the bride of God, so she could be with her Bridegroom.

For the life of the flesh is in the blood, and I have given it for you on the altar to make atonement for your souls, for it is the blood that makes atonement by the life.

Leviticus 17:11

CELEBRATION

And I adorned you with ornaments and put bracelets on your wrists and a chain on your neck. And I put a ring on your nose and earrings in your ears and a beautiful crown on your head.

Ezekiel 16:11-12

Seven is an important number in the Lord's eyes and seems to represent completion. So, once the bride and groom reach their home, a seven-day celebration would be held in their honor. In Exodus 34, after Moses comes down from the mountain of God to find the Israelites worshiping an idol, God renews His covenant with them.

And he said, "Behold, I am making a covenant. Before all your people I will do marvels, such as have not been created in all the earth or in any nation. And all the people among whom you are shall see the work of the LORD, for it is an awesome thing that I will do with you.

Exodus 34:10

A wedding feast is about demonstrating the family's excitement over the new relationship that has been created. God, likewise, wants to display His delight in His people and their relationship. In Exodus 34, God goes on to reiterate that they cannot make gods for themselves because He is a jealous God. He also institutes three feasts that all male Israelites are to take part in every year. Each feast lasts seven days. There was the Feast of Unleavened Bread, to commemorate their miraculous exodus from Egypt; the Feast of Weeks, where they offer the first fruits of their wheat harvest to the Lord in thanks; and the Feast of Ingathering at the year's end. Throughout their generations, these celebrations would remind the Israelites of their relationship with the Lord and be a witness to the nations surrounding them that they were God's people.

> **The feasts were as anniversaries are today: a time to focus on the relationship and renew the love a couple has for each other. What feast do we partake today to commemorate our relationship with the Lord, and why does it matter?**

_____

_____

_____

LOVE SONGS

Throughout Jewish history, the Song of Songs was celebrated and loved, but as modern Christians we often shake our heads at the descriptions and content. All songs and poems lose their significance when translated because either the meaning or the rhyming scheme must be sacrificed. Also, different cultures attach different values to comparisons. Most phrases in songs and poems are not meant to be taken literally. They are meant to convey a feeling. For example, the lyrics to Dolly Parton's song "Jolene,"

Your beauty is beyond compare
With flaming locks of auburn hair
With ivory skin and eyes of emerald green
Your smile is like a breath of spring
Your voice is soft like summer rain
And I cannot compete with you, Jolene.

Can you imagine how this song could be misconstrued if the lyrics were translated into another language and given to people of a vastly different culture? This is the main reason I believe the Song of Solomon is so confusing to us.

Ultimately the Song of Songs is a love song. The title, "The Song of Songs, which is Solomon's" doesn't necessarily mean that Solomon is the writer, but that it was written during the time or in the style of Solomon. My Bible has titles in the book added by translators like, "Solomon and His Bride Delight in Each Other." However, there are many arguments against Solomon being the male voice in the songs. One is that the man in these songs is a shepherd, not a king. Another is that in chapter three, when the bride describes seeing Solomon, she speaks of him as "King Solomon," while before she spoke of her beloved as "you/your." The song seems to be written during Solomon's reign, the golden age of the Jewish nation; therefore, it would be customary to include references to their great king. Solomon, in his extreme wealth, would be a source for comparison and poetic language like in Matthew 6:29, when Jesus compared Solomon's splendor to the lilies of the field.

> **Poetry of this kind was very common during this time period, so why are we so uncomfortable talking about the contents of the Song of Solomon?**

_____

_____

_____

Think of some of your favorite movies. Why do you love them? Whether it's a comedy, drama, or an action flick, I am betting that it involves a love story. Nearly every movie has one, and that's because we view romance as a central theme in all important stories. We are designed with the desire to love, be loved, and to share that love through intimacy with our husband. To fully appreciate and understand the Song of Solomon, you must take yourself back to the time where you were the heroine in your own love story. I am taking liberty to set the stage for you through this short story. Once again, put yourself into the shoes of a young Hebrew girl.

A young man comes to your family to trade with your father. You linger in doorways and watch as he makes your brothers laugh and your father smile. You catch him watching you as you bring water to your mother. He soon finds ways to help you with your chores, whether it's carrying your basket of grapes from the garden or escorting you and your sister as you bring bread and water to your brothers in the fields. He is a wonderful storyteller. He describes his home in the fertile valleys of the South and tells you about the places he's traveled. You feel your face grow warm whenever he approaches, and you hope he feels something for you as well.

One day your father calls you to walk with him in your family's vineyard. He asks you what you think of the trader, and you shyly speak a word or two in his favor.

"Would you want to be his wife?" he asks.

You inhale quickly and hold your breath. You look up at your father's bearded face. He is smiling. He approves. "Yes, I would."

He finds you in the garden. You are alone among the vines, hidden from the house and the fields. You were hoping he would search for you here. You hear him approaching from behind, but you don't turn around. You know your face will betray too much. He slides his hands around your waist and holds you against him.

"Have you spoken to your father?"

"Yes," you whisper.

"So, have I." He leans down and kisses your neck and turns you around.

You sit at the place of honor at the great feast thrown by your father. Your husband holds your hand and smiles at you. You feel as if the world is slipping away because the next day, he must leave and return to his home. Though you are married, you will not share his bed until he returns to bring you to his father's house. For a year, you lie awake longing for your husband. With the money he has given for you, you buy new clothes and ointments. You rise before dawn to begin your chores to avoid the harsh midday sun. You want to be radiant for your beloved. The rains come, and the rains cease, and soon, the vineyards are ripe again. You wait every evening, hoping to hear his voice calling for you. Everything is ready, and you long for him to come.

Now you are ready to read the Song of Solomon. Go ahead and read the eight short chapters with your most open-minded attitude.

The opening line is, "Let him kiss me with the kisses of his mouth! For your love is better than wine." This book is about a bride awaiting her husband and her delight in being the object of his affection. Descriptions like "my hands dripped with myrrh" in 5:5 should not be taken literally, but to express feeling. In her excitement to open the door to her beloved, her hands felt like they were coated with expensive spices. The descriptions of grapes, fawns, and towers are sensual because that is how marriage is designed to be. Husband and wife should delight in each other and long to be together.

Do the descriptions of fruit, animals, and nature remind you of another biblical couple? What would the significance be in alluding to them?

_____

_____

_____

Throughout the songs, the writer has praised and admired Solomon, but what does Chapter 8:11-12 indicate (understanding that the vineyards are a metaphor for women)?

_____

_____

_____

These songs invite us to imagine what it would be like to able to love and be loved within the safety of the Garden of Eden. How would our marriages change if there was no shame, guilt, or fear? How about our relationship with God?

Write down these verses:

Isaiah 54:10 _____

_____

_____

_____

_____

_____

Jeremiah 31:3 _____

_____

_____

_____

John 15:9 _____

_____

_____

_____

Do you long for the Lord with the same passion as the bride? He longs for you that much and more.

> And now, Israel, what does the LORD your God require of you, but to fear the LORD your God, to walk in all his ways, to love him, to serve the LORD your God with all your heart and with all your soul, and to keep the commandments and statutes of the LORD, which I am commanding you today for your good? Behold, to the LORD your God belong heaven and the heaven of heavens, the earth with all that is in it. Yet the LORD set his heart in love on your fathers and chose their offspring after them, you above all peoples, as you are this day.
> Deuteronomy 10:12-15

The Song of Solomon is a representation of the love God desires between Himself and Israel, His bride. This is also the love

He wants between Him and you.

> Set me as a seal upon your heart, as a seal upon your arm, for love is strong as death, jealousy is fierce as the grave. Its flashes are flashes of fire, the very flame of the LORD. Many waters cannot quench love, neither can floods drown it. If a man offered for love all the wealth of his house, he would be utterly despised.
> Song of Solomon 8:6-7

We often think of our relationship with God as being between a parent and a child. How does Song of Solomon change that?

_____

_____

_____

5

THE UNFAITHFUL WIFE

You shall make no covenant with them and their gods.
They shall not dwell in your land, lest they make you
sin against me; for if you serve their gods, it will surely be a snare to you.

Exodus 23:32-33

ome have said that the death of a spouse is easier
to bear than finding out they have been unfaithful.
To bind yourself to someone only to find out they
have left you for another is a hurt I am blessed to
have never experienced, but God knows that pain. Nearly a fourth
of the Old Testament speaks of the same thing: The Lord calling his
people back from their habitual unfaithfulness. God sends prophet after prophet threatening, pleading, and begging his people to
come back to him, promising forgiveness if they will just return.

In chapter 3, I asked you to read the first part of Ezekiel 16. Now, read more of the story starting in verse 15 and stopping at verse 43.

God makes three accusations against Israel: they gave God's gifts to idols, they made "lofty places" to worship those idols, and they formed alliances with foreign countries. These things are all described as adultery. Let's see why.

According to the law of Moses, a husband was required to provide his wife with three things: clothes, food, and sex (Exodus 21:10). God claims he richly provided these things for His people, but instead of cherishing these gifts and praising Him, they gave them to their idols.

> And you took your embroidered garments to cover them, and set my oil and my incense before them. Also my bread that I gave you—I fed you with fine flour and oil and honey—you set before them for a pleasing aroma; and so it was, declares the Lord GOD. And you took your sons and your daughters, whom you had borne to me, and these you sacrificed to them to be devoured. Were your whorings so small a matter that you slaughtered my children and delivered them up as an offering by fire to them?
>
> Ezekiel 16:18-21

Examine your life for a moment. God has richly given us many gifts beyond food, clothing, and family. Are we using these blessings for God's glory? Or, like Israel, are we placing these gifts at the feet of idols?

_____

_____

Few things are as shocking as human sacrifice, much less child sacrifice. Who are these gods that demand such things, and why did the Israelites serve them? When we think of the idols that lured the Israelites away, we tend to think foremost of Ba'al. "Ba'al" is a Hebrew word that means "master" or "husband," so it can be used as a title as well as a specific name. Ba'al was a fertility god and the chief of the Canaanite deities. In times of distress, like poor harvest or war, worshipers sacrificed their children to him in hopes he would once again bless the land. The Israelites spent forty years wandering the wilderness as nomadic shepherds and may have been tempted by the belief that they needed to worship the god who had blessed Canaan with such fruitfulness to ensure its continuance. In 2 Chronicles 28, we read of Ahaz, the king of Judah, worshiping this false god in the Hinnom Valley, which is on the southern slope of Jerusalem—within sight of the Temple. The Valley of Hinnom is also known as "Gehenna," which is interpreted as "hell" because of the curse that lies upon it from Ahaz's acts (Jeremiah 21:2-6).

> But he walked in the ways of the kings of Israel. He even made metal images for the Baals, and he made offerings in the Valley of the Son of Hinnom and burned his sons as an offering, according to the abominations of the nations whom the LORD drove out before the people of Israel.
>
> 2 Chronicles 28:2-3

The word "Ba'al" is a title that can be combined with other words to mean "master of." It is also translated as "husband" in many places throughout the Law of Moses. Yet, God never refers to himself as a "Ba'al/master" except in this one verse. "And in that day, declares the Lord, you will call me 'My Husband,' and no longer will you call me 'My Ba'al.'" Hosea 2:16. How did the Israelites see God, and how did God want to be seen? How do we see God versus how He wants to be seen?

_____

_____

_____

Molech was another Canaanite god the Israelites worshiped. Molech's statues had a large oven at the base that worshipers would offer their sacrifices—including their children. In 1 Kings 11:7, we read that Solomon built a temple for Molech along with other gods. Historians argue about whether Molech was a god's name or whether it was a type of sacrifice meaning to give the most precious thing you possess in hopes of earning a god's favor. Either way, the practice was obviously despicable. God calls out this atrocity specifically in the Law of Moses:

> Say to the people of Israel, Any one of the people of Israel or of the strangers who sojourn in Israel who gives any of his children to Molech shall surely be put to death. The people of the land shall stone him

with stones. I myself will set my face against that man and will cut him off from among his people, because he has given one of his children to Molech, to make my sanctuary unclean and to profane my holy name. And if the people of the land do at all close their eyes to that man when he gives one of his children to Molech, and do not put him to death, then I will set my face against that man and against his clan and will cut them off from among their people, him and all who follow him in whoring after Molech.

Leviticus 20:2-5

How does abortion compare to child sacrifice? What sins do we "close our eyes to"?

The Israelites' adultery was not only metaphorical but literal. The second accusation regards the "lofty place" they built, which is a reference to the worship of Asherah, the supposed mother and lover of Ba'al. To appease the goddess, her worshipers would congregate around a carved wooden pole or tree to perform sex acts. Here worshipers pay to use male or female prostitutes as a form of worship (Hosea 4:13-14). Jezebel worshiped Asherah and supported 400 Asherah prophets (1 Kings 18:19). In Deuteronomy 23:17, we read, "None of the daughters of Israel shall be a cult prostitute, and none of the sons of Israel shall be a cult prostitute." Among the Canaanites, however, the selling of a child into cult prostitution was accepted and thought to bring favor from the gods.

> **Does knowing the practices of the Canaanites and how they affected the Israelites help you better understand why God ordered the Israelites to wipe them out completely upon entering the promised land and why God forbade marriage to foreigners? Read the difficult passages of Numbers 25:1-13 and Ezra 9:1-10:4.**

_____

_____

_____

The last accusation against Israel was that they sought alliances with the Egyptians, Assyrians, and Chaldeans. God commanded his people never to return to Egypt (Deuteronomy 17:16), yet from the time of Solomon, God's people intermarried, traded, and allied in war (Solomon's first recorded wife was an Egyptian Princess in 1 Kings 3:1). Israel and Judah paid tribute money to the neighboring superpowers hoping to prevent their invasion. This is what the Lord refers to whenever he mentions his wife offering payments to her lovers.

> Judah has been faithless, and abomination has been committed in Israel and in Jerusalem. For Judah has profaned the sanctuary of the LORD, which he loves,

and has married the daughter of a foreign god.
Malachi 2:11

In Ezekiel 8, we read of how God took Ezekiel in the Spirit to His Temple in Jerusalem. There he shows Ezekiel how even the priests were consumed in idol worship. There was an altar to an idol set up in the inner courtyard next to the altar of the Lord, there were idols in the personal rooms of the priests, and the entire body of priests on duty, including the High Priest, were worshiping the sun. The Temple was intended to be God's special place to dwell with His people, the equivalent of a marriage bed, but they grossly defiled it. And God was ready to pronounce judgment

> And I will judge you as women who commit adultery and shed blood are judged, and bring upon you the blood of wrath and jealousy. And I will give you into their hands, and they shall throw down your vaulted chamber and break down your lofty places. They shall strip you of your clothes and take your beautiful jewels and leave you naked and bare. They shall bring up a crowd against you, and they shall stone you and cut you to pieces with their swords. And they shall burn your houses and execute judgments upon you in the sight of many women. I will make you stop playing the whore, and you shall also give payment no more. So will I satisfy my wrath on you, and my jealousy shall depart from you. I will be calm and will no more be angry.
> Ezekiel 16:38-42

The judgment against an adulterous wife is from Leviticus 20:10, "If a man commits adultery with the wife of his neighbor, both the adulterer and the adulteress shall surely be put to death." Notice also that the Lord will punish his bride by using her "lovers," but according to the law, they must both be punished. Isaiah, Jeremiah, and Ezekiel prophesy about the coming destruction of Egypt, Assyria, and Chaldea (Babylon), and history tells us that these prophesies were all fulfilled.

> In Numbers 5:11-31, we read of the strange test for a woman accused of committing adultery. A cup of water mixed with dust from the floor of the tabernacle is given to test a wife's virtue. Throughout the prophets, God says His people will drink a cup of judgment (Isaiah 51:17, Jeremiah 25:15-17, Ezekiel 23:32-34). In fact, we drink this cup of judgment every week. Read and meditate on 1 Corinthians 11:27-32. How should this change the way you take this cup?

_____

_____

_____

Though God's people grossly adulterated their relationship, God refuses to abandon the covenant He made with them.

> For thus says the Lord GOD: I will deal with you as you have done, you who have despised the oath in breaking the covenant, yet I will remember my covenant with you in the days of your youth, and I will establish for you an everlasting covenant [...] that you may remember and be confounded, and never open

your mouth again because of your shame, when I atone for you for all that you have done, declares the Lord GOD.

Ezekiel 16:59-60, 63

In Isaiah, the Bible's largest collection of prophecies, we find a pattern of judgment, punishment, and the promise of redemption. The promise is that a remnant will survive the terrible wrath God wreaks on His people and return to the Lord. Only then, can the sign be given that the covenant is still intact and the whole purpose of God's oath to Abraham be fulfilled.

Therefore the Lord himself will give you a sign. Behold, the virgin shall conceive and bear a son, and shall call his name Immanuel.

Isaiah 7:14

Immanuel means "God is with us." The purpose of marriage is to bring children into the world, and most importantly, an Heir to fulfill the will of the Father.

Throughout the prophets, God repeatedly mentions the reason His people have gone astray is their lack of knowledge about Him and His Word. How is this still true today?

_____

_____

_____

THE HEARTBROKEN HUSBAND

he sun pours in his window, but he is already awake. Hosea turns away from the empty place next to him and watches the sky lighten from purple to pink. He wonders in whose bed she is waking. Anger bubbles to the surface for a moment as he quickly gets out of bed. Hosea goes to the window, wanting to scream in frustration, but the three prone forms across the room catch his eye. Her children, who he hopes are his children, still sleep peacefully. Their names, foretold by God, cannot be uttered without recalling the faithlessness of their mother. Jezreel, the firstborn, is named after the evil King Ahab's stronghold that God has vowed to break. The girl is named Loruhamah, meaning, "No mercy" because God has said he will have no more mercy on the house of Israel. Hosea runs his fingers through his graying hair as he looks down at his second son, the youngest child, nestled between his siblings. He will have to be a strong man to endure his name, Loammi, which means "not my people." It is a name for an illegitimate son—a rejected son. *These are the names God has chosen for Hosea's children and for His people because He has been abandoned just as Hosea has been abandoned.*

The cries of worshipers call out to Ba'al as they do every morning. Before the sun reaches midday, the marketplace will be flooded with people buying gifts for the various shrines and idols around the city. Hosea sighs and wipes tears from his eyes.

Why did God ask Hosea to marry Gomer? How does God use our heartache for His purpose? Is the saying true that we are never given more than we can bear?

_____

_____

_____

At the time of Hosea's prophecies, Israel in the North had been split from Judah for around 200 years and was being ruled by King Jeroboam II. Idolatry was rampant, and God's covenant was forgotten. Hosea was sent by God to warn the people of the coming disaster that will take place in only a few decades. Hosea also intimately understands God's struggle in what to do with Israel. In Hosea 1:2 we read, "When the Lord first spoke through Hosea, the Lord said to Hosea, 'Go, take to yourself a wife of whoredom and have children of whoredom, for the land commits great whoredom by forsaking the Lord.'" Hosea obeys and marries Gomer and has three children by her. Because she was known to be a prostitute, Hosea would have most likely had to take his children to the elders of the city and legally adopt them because his parentage would always be in question.

After Gomer has her third child, she seems to run away with another man. Hosea experiences the same anguish and anger of the Lord. According to the law, Hosea would have been within his rights to stone his wife. If he didn't want to go that far, he could have divorced her or sold her and her children into slavery. These are the same choices the Lord wrestles with regarding what he should do with Israel.

> Plead with your mother, plead— for she is not my wife, and I am not her husband— that she put away her whoring from her face, and her adultery from between her breasts; lest I strip her naked and make her as in the day she was born, and make her like a wilderness, and make her like a parched land, and kill her with thirst. Upon her children also I will have no mercy, because they are children of whoredom.
>
> Hosea 2:2-4

The phrase, "she is not my wife and I am not her husband," is thought to be the language the Jews used when writing a certificate of divorce. However, God continues with a different plan.

> Therefore I will hedge up her way with thorns, and I will build a wall against her, so that she cannot find her paths. She shall pursue her lovers but not overtake them, and she shall seek them but shall not find them. Then she shall say, "I will go and return to my first husband, for it was better for me then than now."
>
> Hosea 2:6-7

In Matthew 19:9, we read that divorce and remarriage is only allowed if the spouse has committed adultery. How does this exception reflect God's character? Does God use this exception for His relationship with His people?

_____

_____

_____

Because the LORD was witness between you and the wife of your youth, to whom you have been faithless, though she is your companion and your wife by covenant. Did he not make them one, with a portion of the Spirit in their union? And what was the one God seeking? Godly offspring. So guard yourselves in your spirit, and let none of you be faithless to the wife of your youth. "For the man who does not love his wife but divorces her, says the LORD, the God of Israel, covers his garment with violence, says the LORD of hosts. So guard yourselves in your spirit, and do not be faithless."

Malachi 2:14b-16

God still wants Israel back. Even after all they have done, He still loves them. Hosea continues prophesying and says that Israel will be punished. She will lose all the blessings that God has given her, but she will learn to love Him again and forget the gods that lured her astray.

I will betroth you to Me forever; Yes, I will betroth you to Me In righteousness and justice, In lovingkindness and mercy; I will betroth you to Me in faithfulness, And you shall know the LORD.

Hosea 2:19-20 NKJV

Next, Hosea lives out God's dream of being reunited with his bride.

And the LORD said to me, "Go again, love a woman who is loved by another man and is an adulteress, even as the LORD loves the children of Israel, though they turn to other gods and love cakes of raisins."

Hosea 3:1

Hosea buys her from the man she has prostituted herself to, and he tells her, "You must dwell as mine for many days. You shall not play the whore, or belong to another man; so will I also be to you." In Hosea 3:2, we read that Hosea bought her for 15 shekels of silver and five bushels of barley. The listing of the price is significant because the need for adding grain indicates that he spent all his money, and that was still not enough to buy her. He did not buy her out of his abundance, he spent all he had to get her back.

In Hosea, we read how discipline and love go hand in hand. Read 1 Samuel 15:22, Hosea 6:6-7, and John 14:15. From the beginning, we have sought to go our own way and ask for forgiveness when our choices catch up with us. How does viewing our relationship with God as a marriage help us be more obedient?

_____

_____

_____

_____

How lonely sits the city that was full of people! How like a widow has she become, she who was great among the nations! She who was a princess among the provinces has become a slave.

Lamentations 1:1

The Lord chooses to forgive his people, but only after they realize the terrible consequences for their actions. In 587 B.C., the coming judgment culminates in the destruction of the Temple by King Nebuchadnezzar of Babylon. God's people are killed by famine, plague, and the sword. Those that survive are taken into captivity. However, while in captivity, they see amazing signs that God has not abandoned them. Read these chapters and write how God showed His people that He had not given up on them.

Ezekiel 43 _____

_____

Daniel 3 _____

_____

Daniel 5 _____

_____

Daniel 6 _____

_____

Ezra 1 _____

_____

Esther 8 _____

_____

Ezekiel prophesies of a new temple and the glory of the Lord returning. Three men defy the king and survive the fiery furnace. A hand writes on the wall of the king when he uses the instruments from the Temple, pronouncing his judgment, and the king dies that very night. A captive rises to the second-highest office in the Empire and miraculously survives an assassination attempt. Babylon is overthrown by Persia, whose king allows the captives to take their holy treasures from the Temple back to Jerusalem and rebuild. Those that remain in Babylon are saved from genocide when the queen reveals herself to be a Jewess.

> Behold, the days are coming, declares the LORD, when I will make a new covenant with the house of Israel and the house of Judah, not like the covenant that I made with their fathers on the day when I took them by the hand to bring them out of the land of Egypt, my covenant that they broke, though I was their husband, declares the LORD. For this is the covenant that I will make with the house of Israel after those days, declares the LORD: I will put my law within them, and I will write it on their hearts. And I will be their God, and they shall be my people. And no longer shall each one teach his neighbor and each his brother, saying, 'Know the LORD,' for they shall

all know me, from the least of them to the greatest, declares the LORD. For I will forgive their iniquity, and I will remember their sin no more.

Jeremiah 31:31-34

Lamentations is so named for the great lament that went up among all Jews at the destruction of the Temple and the removal from their homeland. However, the central verses in the book are,

The steadfast love of the LORD never ceases; his mercies never come to an end; they are new every morning; great is your faithfulness. "The LORD is my portion," says my soul, "therefore I will hope in him."

Lamentations 3:22-24

Finally, the remnant of God's people that remain is ready to come home.

When Israel was a child, I loved him, and out of Egypt I called my son. The more they were called, the more they went away; they kept sacrificing to the Baals and burning offerings to idols. Yet it was I who taught Ephraim to walk; I took them up by their arms, but they did not know that I healed them. [...] How can I give you up, O Ephraim? How can I hand you over, O Israel? How can I make you like Admah? How can I treat you like Zeboiim? My heart recoils within me; my compassion grows warm and tender. I will not execute my burning anger; I will not again destroy Ephraim; for I am God and not a man, the Holy One in your midst, and I will not come in wrath.

Hosea 11:1-3, 8-9

How does this passage point to the cross?

_____

_____

_____

REDEEMED

For where you go, I will go, and where you lodge, I will lodge. Your people shall be my people, and your God my God. Where you die, I will die and there will I be buried. May the Lord do so to me and more also if anything but death parts me from you.

Ruth 1:16b-17

This passage is one of the most commonly quoted scriptures at weddings, yet these words pass between daughter-in-law and mother-in-law. There is no bond of blood, no physical attraction, nothing for Ruth to gain in this relationship. There is just commitment.

> **Study Matthew 8:18-22 and Luke 14:25-33. What are the costs of being committed to Jesus? How committed are you?**

_____

_____

_____

We all love stories. The best stories are the ones that have a moral just far enough beneath the surface that we feel it without seeing it at first glance. Ruth is such a story. I believe these four chapters sum up the entire Old Testament and reveal a secret about the kingdom of God that completely baffled the Jews. I invite you to read the book of Ruth now.

Though the book is titled "Ruth," I hope you notice that the story is really about Naomi. Naomi was a member of the tribe of Judah and a wife with two sons. When famine strikes the land, Naomi's family leaves and goes to the foreign country of Moab, instead of staying and trusting God will take care of them. Naomi symbolically walks the path of the people of God. In times of trial, the Israelites seek out the help of foreigners and idols rather than relying on God, and tragedy follows. Naomi's husband and two sons die, one after the other, without leaving heirs to carry on the family name or take care of Naomi in her old age. This is the worst calamity that can befall a woman at that time. Naomi claims that "the hand of the Lord has gone out against me." And certainly, it had for her as it will later for the nations of Israel and Judah. God abandons them all due to their unfaithfulness, but He is not done with them.

When a woman marries, her allegiance shifts to her husband's family. Therefore, Orpah and Ruth stay with their mother-in-law. Naomi reasonably suggests that they return home, thereby dissolving the tie that binds them to her family. Orpah returns, but Ruth remains faithful. God saw the same happen with Israel and Judah. The northern tribes that formed the nation of Israel were not brought out of bondage like the nation of Judah. They were too polluted with idolatry to cry out to God in their distress. They believed their best hope was to take their own path, as Orpah did.

> **In 1 Kings 12, the kingdom of Israel divided under the rule of Solomon's son, Rehoboam. Starting in verse 25, Jeroboam set up two idols for the northern tribes to worship to prevent the people from returning to Jerusalem. God instituted three feasts that all males were required to attend to keep the people united in worship. Jeroboam, however, knew that he would lose his kingdom if the people knew the Lord. What idols has Satan set up today in order to divide us and keep us from being a part of God's kingdom?**

_____

_____

_____

Naomi and Ruth return to Bethlehem, where they find their family land desolate. They have no means to buy seed and no way to work the fields even if they did. Ruth chooses a nearby field and asks permission to glean behind the harvesters (Leviticus 19:9-10). The owner of the field, Boaz, takes notice and ensures her safety by commanding his men not to touch her and telling her to stay in his fields. He lets her eat a midday meal with him and his reapers and even tells his men to pull out some of the barley they have already cut to leave for her. Due to Boaz's generosity, after she threshed out her grain, she had the equivalent to twenty-two liters of barley. Naomi left during a famine and came back to find God providing for her and Ruth in their destitution, out of the field of a kinsman, no less—the field of a redeemer.

A kinsman-redeemer is a close male relative whose duty is to help a family member in times of trouble. In Leviticus 25:47-49, we read that if a man is forced to sell himself into slavery, then one of his relatives can redeem him by buying him from his master. In Deuteronomy 25:5-10, we read about Levirate marriage or "marriage to one's brother-in-law." The Law states that if brothers dwell together and one of them dies, leaving no son, then the brother will marry his sister-in-law in order to provide an heir for his brother. In marrying her, the brother would be under obligation to provide clothes, food, and protection for his brother's wife and children. If a brother refuses to do this, he would be publicly shamed and known as "the man who does not build up his brother's house." A man could have many reasons for not wanting to marry his sister-in-law. There would be a significant financial responsibility. If his brother had no heir, then his brother's land and inheritance would become his (this was the motivation for Onan's sin in Genesis 38:6-10). Naomi and Ruth would have been even less desirable because Naomi was probably past child-bearing years, and Ruth was a foreigner from the hated nation of Moab.

> **Levirate laws have not applied to the Israelites since they entered captivity. However, what do these laws teach us regarding God's intentions for His people?**

▌ Read 1 Corinthians 12:26 and James 1:27.

_____

_____

_____

Naomi tells Ruth, "My daughter, should I not seek rest for you, that it may be well with you?" (Ruth 3:1 NKJV). Naomi tells Ruth to wash and anoint herself as a bride would before her wedding and go to the threshing floor that night. As darkness falls around the celebrating men, Ruth creeps up just outside the circle of light. She waits for them to fall asleep and "came softly and uncovered his feet and lay down" (Ruth 3:7). In the middle of the night, Boaz realizes that there is a woman at his feet, and Ruth tells him, "I am Ruth, your servant. Spread your wings over your servant for you are a redeemer," (Ruth 3:9).

▌ What is the significance of the phrase "spread your wings over your servant?" Go back to Ezekiel 16:8.

_____

_____

_____

This act was most likely a part of the wedding ceremony, a symbol of the husband bringing the bride under his protection. Boaz graciously agrees.

May you be blessed by the LORD, my daughter. You have made this last kindness greater than the first in that you have not gone after young men, whether poor or rich. And now, my daughter, do not fear. I will do for you all that you ask, for all my fellow townsmen know that you are a worthy woman.

Ruth 3:10-11

By the language Boaz uses, he seems to be much older than Ruth. He was aware of his connection with her and Naomi as their redeemer but perhaps was worried that she would not desire such an older husband. The two kindnesses he is referring to in verse 10 are her loyalty to her husband's family by taking care of Naomi and seeking a marriage within the family clan to continue her husband's family name.

In the morning, Boaz goes to the city gate, where the town elders handle matters of business. The other family redeemer that had a closer tie is called over.

Then he said to the redeemer, "Naomi, who has come back from the country of Moab, is selling the parcel of land that belonged to our relative Elimelech. So I thought I would tell you of it and say, 'Buy it in the presence of those sitting here and in the presence of the elders of my people.' If you will redeem it, redeem it. But if you will not, tell me, that I may know, for there is no one besides you to redeem it, and I come after you." And he said, "I will redeem it."

Ruth 4:3-4

In Leviticus 25:23-31, we read the laws surrounding the selling of land. The land is tied in with one's tribe and clan and was not to be sold to outsiders. If the land was sold, it was to be returned to the seller in the year of Jubilee, which occurred every 50 years (Leviticus 25:1-4). Boaz strategically mentioned only Naomi's name when putting forward the transaction, knowing that his kinsman would be thinking that Naomi was an old, childless widow, therefore in Jubilee, there would be no one to give the land back to, making it his. This was a deal of a lifetime, he would be crazy not to buy it, but there's a catch.

> Then Boaz said, "The day you buy the field from the hand of Naomi, you also acquire Ruth the Moabite, the widow of the dead, in order to perpetuate the name of the dead in his inheritance." Then the redeemer said, "I cannot redeem it for myself, lest I impair my own inheritance."
>
> Ruth 4:5-6a

The land belongs to Elimelech's family, so in buying it, he is obligated to fulfill the duties of a Levirate marriage to continue the family's name. The land could only be used for his profit until the year of Jubilee when it would have to be returned. And as Ruth's husband, he would have to provide for her, Naomi, and any children Ruth has by him.

Boaz, however, redeems them and makes an oral covenant before the elders of the city saying that he is buying from Naomi, the land from Elimelech's family. He also says he is buying Ruth with the intention of perpetuating the name of her dead husband. My interpretation is that Boaz will pay Naomi the cost of the land, as well as a bride price for Ruth, and take them both into his household. The elders bless Boaz's marriage with what was probably the customary blessing bestowed on couples at their wedding,

> May the LORD make the woman, who is coming into
> your house, like Rachel and Leah, who together built
> up the house of Israel. May you act worthily in Ephra-
> thah and be renowned in Bethlehem, and may your
> house be like the house of Perez, whom Tamar bore
> to Judah, because of the offspring that the LORD will
> give you by this young woman.
>
> Ruth 4:11b-12

A very different tale regarding Levirate marriage is found in Genesis 38. What are the differences between that story and this one?

_____

_____

_____

Boaz then takes Ruth into his house and consummates their marriage, and she bears a son. This son will carry on Elimelech's family name, inherit his family's portion of land, and care for his mother and grandmother in their old age. The women of Bethlehem praise the Lord,

> Blessed be the LORD, who has not left you this day
> without a redeemer, and may his name be renowned
> in Israel! He shall be to you a restorer of life and a
> nourisher of your old age, for your daughter-in-law

who loves you, who is more to you than seven sons,
has given birth to him.

Ruth 4:14-15

Having a son was believed to be a sign of God's blessing, so
having seven (a sign of perfection) sons was the loftiest goal a woman could achieve, yet the women said Ruth is more valuable. They
name her son Obed, which means "servant" in honor of Ruth's ser-
vice to Naomi.

The close of the book shows the significance of the story, "He
(Obed) was the father of Jesse, the father of David" (Ruth 4:17b).
In those fields that once lay fallow, a young boy would one day run
from watching his sheep to be anointed king. Much later, God's
people leave their fields after years of disobedience in the hands of
their enemies. However, God goes with them, and eventually, after
much sorrow and loss, brings them back. Like Naomi, they find
their land desolate, but a Redeemer is coming. Another boy from
Bethlehem that will one day be King. The Israelites deeply desire
to have their Savior come, but what they don't realize is that there
is another bride that is also waiting: Ruth. The Moabitess, the foreigner, the gentile.

Behold my servant, whom I uphold, my chosen, in
whom my soul delights; I have put my Spirit upon
him; he will bring forth justice to the nations.

Isaiah 42:1

**How is Boaz like Jesus? How are the Israelites like
Naomi? How are the gentiles like Ruth?**

THE BRIDEGROOM COMES

Behold, the virgin shall conceive and bear a son, and shall call his name Immanuel.

Isaiah 7:14

Now the birth of Jesus Christ took place in this way. When his mother Mary had been betrothed to Joseph, before they came together she was found to be with child from the Holy Spirit.

Matthew 1:18

She will bear a son, and you shall call his name Jesus, for he will save his people from their sins.

Matthew 1:21

*I*mmanuel means, "God is with us." Jesus is the Greek form of the Hebrew name, Yeshua, meaning "Yahweh saves." Just like the promised child to Abraham, Jesus is the promised Savior. Prophecy, the virgin birth, and His God-given name show us He is clearly God's literal Son and is here with a great purpose: to seek and save the lost (Luke 19:10). However, before the Son comes, a messenger is sent, just as Abraham sent his servant to seek out a wife for his son.

> "Behold, I send My messenger, And he will prepare the way before Me. And the Lord, whom you seek, Will suddenly come to His temple, Even the Messenger of the covenant, In whom you delight. Behold, He is coming," Says the LORD of hosts.
> Malachi 3:1 NKJV

> John came baptizing in the wilderness and preaching a baptism of repentance for the remission of sins.
> Mark 1:4 NKJV

> He said: "I am 'The voice of one crying in the wilderness: "Make straight the way of the LORD," ' as the prophet Isaiah said." Now those who were sent were from the Pharisees. And they asked him, saying, "Why then do you baptize if you are not the Christ, nor Elijah, nor the Prophet?"
> John 1:23-25 NKJV

As modern-day Christians, we once again are missing out on an important piece of Jewish culture: baptism. The Greek word "baptismah" has been transliterated to our word "baptism," which means "immersion." Baptizing oneself or being baptized for spiritual reasons was a regular part of Jewish life. According to the Law of Moses, if one had touched something unclean or had been sick, they had to be baptized either in a river, spring, or man-made mikveh (a carved-out, spring-fed pool with steps, built for the purpose of immersion). Before entering the Temple complex, conservative worshippers would baptize themselves just in case they had inadvertently become unclean. These were not simple baths; they removed uncleanness that separated them from God. All Jews baptized themselves before Yom Kippur, the day of atonement when the High Priest went into the Holy of Holies to sacrifice for their sins. Another significant time someone would need to be baptized was before starting a new chapter in their life. Converts to Judaism would be baptized to signify their change as would a bride and groom before their marriage.

> **Study John 1:29-34 and 3:28-29. Why was Jesus baptized?**

_____

_____

_____

In the beginning was the Word, and the Word was with God, and the Word was God.

John 1:1

The significance of Jesus being the Word or Will of God is that He represents God's covenant with his people. "Do not think

I have come to abolish the Law or the Prophets; I have not come to abolish them but to fulfill them" (Matthew 5:17). Everything Jesus does is done with the purpose of restoring God's people to the relationship they had with Him in the Garden of Eden. He heals the sick. He forgives sin. He preaches on righteousness. He raises the dead. Jesus is God's will manifested as a man on earth. Jesus also seeks to establish a new covenant with His people.

> **Open your Bible to one of my favorite books, Hebrews 8:6-13. What was wrong with the old covenant?**

_____

_____

_____

> **As the old covenant is passing away, we see that Jesus's presence on earth is a unique time in between the judgment of the Mosaic Law and the mercy of the Gospel. Check out John 8:3-11. Why did Jesus not condemn the woman? (Side note: why do you think Jesus was writing in the sand?) Now turn to John 3:17 and 12:47-48. Why did Jesus not judge the world while He was here?**

_____

_____

_____

The image of Jesus we form while reading the Gospels is one of a man who loved people. He reached out to the unworthy. He wept with His friends. He ate with sinners. He also made beautiful promises to His followers about their relationship. These promises are very similar to what I believe a groom would promise his betrothed.

THE PROMISES OF THE BRIDEGROOM

Matthew 11:28-30 _____

_____

_____

_____

John 14:2-3 _____

_____

_____

_____

John 6:37 _____

_____

_____

_____

However, most of Jesus's teachings warn His followers of the cost of joining Him because the bride shares in the fate of the husband.

THE WARNINGS OF THE BRIDEGROOM

Matthew 10:32-33 _____

_____

_____

_____

_____

Matthew 10:37 _____

_____

_____

_____

Matthew 16:24-25 _____

_____

_____

_____

John 15:18-19 _____

_____

_____

_____

When the disciples of John asked Jesus why His disciples do not fast, He told them, "can the wedding guests mourn as long as the Bridegroom is with them? The days will come when the Bridegroom is taken away from them, and then they will fast." Matthew 9:15. While Jesus walked the earth, His disciples desperately hoped for Him to be a king that would free their land from the Romans. However, what they would not learn until after His death is that Jesus's kingdom was not physical, but spiritual. While in the world,

Jesus was courting His bride, but He would soon have to leave. The time for payment was close at hand, and after the price was paid, the Bridegroom must go.

> **Many early Christians believed Jesus would come back during their lifetime. However, two thousand years have passed, and we are still waiting. Does that diminish the promise? Once the covenant is made, how is the marriage viewed in the eyes of the law?**

_____

_____

_____

At the forging of a covenant, a feast would be held to celebrate the union. When God brings the Israelites out of Egypt, He instituted the Feast of Unleavened Bread to commemorate the beginning of His relationship with His people. Likewise, Jesus establishes a new covenant feast with His disciples on the day He pays the price for them. The Jewish day begins at twilight. What we call "the Lord's Supper" was eaten at evening the day of the Passover—the fourteenth day of Abib—the day Jesus would die.

> Now as they were eating, Jesus took bread, and after blessing it broke it and gave it to the disciples, and said, "Take, eat; this is my body." And he took a cup, and when he had given thanks he gave it to them, saying, "Drink of it, all of you, for this is my blood of the covenant, which is poured out for many for the

forgiveness of sins. I tell you I will not drink again of this fruit of the vine until that day when I drink it new with you in my Father's kingdom."

Matthew 26:26-29

We take part in this feast every Sunday when we eat of the Lord's Supper. The absence of leaven represents a sinless entity. Jewish women would take a fork and striate the bread during preparation to ensure even baking. Jesus's body is similarly striped by lashes. The wine not only looks like blood but contains sterilizing properties. Drinking water was unsafe up until modern times, so wine was added to water to cleanse it of impurity. Likewise, Jesus's blood cleanses those who come in contact with it from sin.

> **Read Numbers 15:4-5. How is the grain offering a foreshadowing to Jesus? What is Jesus doing at this Passover with His disciples?**

_____

_____

_____

The Bridegroom has come, and all is ready. The bride has been called, the covenant has been made, and the feast is underway. All that is left is the price to be paid.

9

THE PRICE

We all love the story of Cinderella. A kind, beautiful young woman, placed in terrible circumstances through no fault of her own, is given the chance to attend a royal ball. Her beauty and charm are enhanced by her fairy godmother's magic so that she captures the attention of the prince as soon as he lays eyes on her. He is instantly entranced; however, the magic only lasts until midnight. As the clock strikes twelve, Cinderella must flee to prevent the prince from seeing who she really is. The prince turns the kingdom upside down looking for her, and when he finally finds Cinderella, he marries her even though she is just a servant, and not the princess that she appeared to be. We all want to believe that we are special enough to have a prince fall in love with us, but in comparison to our relationship with Jesus, a more realistic story would sound something like this:

A woman crouches naked, chained to the wall in a fetid cell. She has no beauty, no youth, nothing to garner any sympathy. Her skin is pocked and diseased. She is so dirty, she hardly looks human. Her life has been short, and the time is near for her execution. A shaft of light causes the woman to cover her eyes as the door is opened to her cell. She has grown very used to absolute darkness. When her eyes adjust, she sees a man standing at the top of the stairs with her jailer. The man is obviously someone of great importance. She squirms to cover her body as they approach.

She keeps her head down in shame but feels the man watching her. She can scarcely understand his words when he asks the jailer, "What will it take to get her out?"

As her heart soars, the woman dares to look up at the stranger, but only for a moment. All her hopes are crushed by the jailer's reply, "Oh, only the highest price will do for her. She has done every evil thing that can be imagined and will do it again if you free her."

The woman lies down on the cold ground. She has done every evil thing. Her skin crawls in memory of what she has done. Unforgivable things. Things that no amount of darkness can hide.

The stranger looks at her sadly. In the brief time she looked at him, she determined she does not know him. She covers her face with her filthy hair and gives up all hope.

His voice is soft, but echoes in the close chamber. "I will pay it," he says. "I will pay it all."

For one will scarcely die for a righteous person— though perhaps for a good person one would dare even to die— but God shows his love for us in that while we were still sinners, Christ died for us. Since, therefore, we have now been justified by his blood, much more shall we be saved by him from the wrath of God.

Romans 5:7-9

A great price was paid for us not because we are intrinsically valuable, but because we owed such a great debt.

> Therefore, just as sin came into the world through one man, and death through sin, and so death spread to all men because all sinned—
>
>   Romans 5:12

Let's go back to the beginning. Open your Bible to Genesis 3. What statement is Adam making in naming his wife "Eve"? What is the significance of verse 21? According to verse 22. Why is death a crucial part of God's plan?

Once Adam and Eve were sent from the garden, they quickly realized the repercussions of disobeying God. In Genesis 4 we read of Cain killing his brother out of jealousy and just two chapters later we read,

> The LORD saw that the wickedness of man was great in the earth, and that every intention of the thoughts of his heart was only evil continually. And the LORD regretted that he had made man on the earth, and it grieved him to his heart. So the LORD said, "I will blot out man whom I have created from the face of the

land, man and animals and creeping things and birds
of the heavens, for I am sorry that I have made them."
Genesis 6:5-7

Mankind without God is a moral black hole. We see this not
only during this time but over and over again throughout history.
"The wages of sin is death..." (Romans 6:23a) and "all have sinned
and fall short of the glory of God" (Romans 3:23). We have a terrible sin problem. However, from the beginning, God has enacted a
plan to save us.

**Who was the first person God made a covenant with?
Turn to Genesis 8:20-22, 9:8-17.**

Through Abraham, God established His people. Through
Moses, God established the Law and a way to atone for sins. For
hundreds of years, the continual sacrifice of animals covered sins,
but it was not enough and was never intended to be the answer.

> For since the law has but a shadow of the good things
> to come instead of the true form of these realities, it
> can never, by the same sacrifices that are continually
> offered every year, make perfect those who draw near.
> Otherwise, would they not have ceased to be offered,
> since the worshipers, having once been cleansed,
> would no longer have any consciousness of sins? But
> in these sacrifices there is a reminder of sins every
> year. For it is impossible for the blood of bulls and
> goats to take away sins.
>
> Hebrews 10:1-4

I believe that in all of us there is an understanding that forgiveness requires sacrifice. We often say when apologizing, "What can I do to make it up to you?" And many pagan religions have incorporated human sacrifice as a way to find forgiveness.

> **Read the account found in Genesis 22:1-14. Where was Abraham supposed to go to sacrifice his son? What is the significance of this place? Check out 2 Chronicles 3:1 and 1 Chronicles 21:14-18, 26-27.**

_____

_____

_____

The Temple was the place where heaven and earth met. Through the veil, in the most holy place, God could dwell only if the people were continually purified with the blood of animals. This was the place for atonement. The great mystery of the ages is that this was the place where God, Himself, would make the ultimate atonement for all of mankind.

> But when Christ appeared as a high priest of the good things that have come, then through the greater and more perfect tent (not made with hands, that is, not of this creation) he entered once for all into the holy places, not by means of the blood of goats and calves but by means of his own blood, thus securing an eternal redemption. For if the blood of goats and bulls, and the sprinkling of defiled persons with the ashes

of a heifer, sanctify for the purification of the flesh, how much more will the blood of Christ, who through the eternal Spirit offered himself without blemish to God, purify our conscience from dead works to serve the living God.

Hebrews 9:11-14

From the moment Adam and Eve sinned, the Lord had a plan. This plan would require a special sacrifice. One that had life and blood, but also eternal power. For God's plan to work, this sacrifice would be for all people from all times: past, present, and future, and be able to remove sin continuously. Thus, this sacrifice had to be a combination of God and man.

Turn to John 19:1-30. Jesus, who existed from the beginning and brought the universe into creation, dies. His heart stops beating, his brain shuts down, and His spirit leaves Him. At this moment, a cataclysmic event happens: the price is paid. What other events happened at the time of Jesus's death, and what do they signify? (Matthew 27:45-54)

_____

_____

_____

THE CONSUMMATION OF THE SPIRIT

> In the beginning God created the heavens and the earth. Now the earth was formless and empty, darkness covered the surface of the watery depths, and the Spirit of God was hovering over the surface of the waters.
>
> Genesis 1:1-2 HCSB

At the dawn of creation, the Spirit of God was there. He is who breathed life into an inanimate world, and through Him, we become truly alive by joining together as one with Jesus Christ.

Who is the Holy Spirit according to 1 Corinthians 2:6-16?

_____

_____

_____

A Jewish couple was considered married once the bride price had been paid. Therefore, once Jesus paid the terrible price our salvation cost, His bride was won. On the first day of the week, the tomb was found empty, but Mary and the others didn't realize Jesus was alive. Turn to John 20:11-23. Verse 22 tells us that Jesus breathed on them and told them to receive the Holy Spirit.

> Then the LORD God formed the man of dust from the ground and breathed into his nostrils the breath of life, and the man became a living creature.
>
> Genesis 2:7

Just as God breathed life into Adam, Jesus breathed his Spirit on those who believed in him. After Jesus was raised from the dead, He met with His disciples for forty short days before the time had come for Him to return to His Father. A bridegroom would spend only a short amount of time after his betrothal with his bride before he too must depart. At this point, the allegory about earthly marriage and our relationship with God differs. We are not left alone to await the coming of our Bridegroom; we are left with His Spirit. At the close of Matthew, Jesus tells His disciples, "And remember I am with you always, to the end of the age." In the upper room on the eve of His death, Jesus tells the eleven, "In a little while the world will see Me no longer, but you will see me. Because I live, you will live too. In that day you will know that I am in My Father, you are in Me, and I am in you" (John 14:19-20).

> **Study Ephesians 1:11-14 and John 16:13-15. How do we come by an inheritance from God? What is needed for an inheritance to be granted?**

When you were betrothed to the Son, you were given the Holy Spirit as a seal. On a written contract, a man's unique seal would be impressed in wax to authenticate the document—the agreement. The Holy Spirit is this seal. He shows that we are God's children through marriage to His Son. He is the down payment, a taste of what is to come. He gives us spiritual gifts, comfort, strength, and hope. And through Him, we are redeemed on the day of judgment. He is who we need to pass the test, to redeem our prize, and to escape the condemnation of death and judgment. However, as in any will or agreement, there are requirements and limits placed on the beneficiaries.

> **Meditate on John 14:15-28. How do we show our love to Jesus? How is Judas's question in verse 22 significant? Why should a bride rejoice at her bridegroom's departure?**

_____

_____

God knew from the beginning that it is not good for man to be alone. Even though a spouse can bring great comfort and joy, there will always be a God-shaped hole within us because we were designed to dwell with the Lord in the garden. Only through our relationship with Jesus, can that hole be filled.

The word *Sabbath* comes from the Hebrew word Shabath, meaning "rest," which is first used in Genesis 2:2-3. "By the seventh day God completed His work that He had done, and He rested on the seventh day from all His work He had done. God blessed the seventh day and declared it holy, for on it He rested from His work of creation" (HCSB). God spent six days making everything we know, and on the seventh day, He simply rested in it. He said, "This is good," and He dwelt there with His creation. After the fall, upon giving His Law to Moses, God reinstated the Sabbath with His people and instituted capital punishment to any who would work on this day.

Why is the observation of the Sabbath not a part of the New Testament Church? Turn to Hebrews 4:1-11.

_____

_____

_____

The Spirit of God has the power to unite us as a body, a church, and a bride. No other force on earth can take people from all walks of life, races, and cultures and unite them so wholly as the Spirit of God. Anywhere that division or dissension can be found is the work of the enemy.

> **Study 1 Corinthians 12:12-26. How does verse 13 point to a Jewish wedding? What is Paul referring to in verses 22-25?**

_____

_____

_____

Our culture teaches us that if we desire something, then we deserve to have it. Phrases like "Follow your heart" and "Do what makes you happy" sound innocent and uplifting, but are not ideas we, as brides of Christ, can live by. The sexual revolution of the sixties is not really a revolution in the sense of anything new, but it was a notable culture shift in the values of our society in the twentieth century. The world that the early church existed in was no different. The Greco-Roman world promoted the idea that the body was made for pleasure. This was the society that had temple prostitutes, gladiatorial games, and slave markets. However, no matter what culture Christians find themselves in, sexual immorality has no place in the body of Christ.

> **Open your Bible to 1 Corinthians 6:12-20. How is sexual immorality sinning against your own body, while other sin is outside your body?**

_____

_____

Contrary to secular opinions, sex is a privilege, not a right, with laws that must be observed if we are to enjoy this gift fully. The same is true of our relationship with the Holy Spirit. Can all the factors be met in a perfect physical relationship without marriage? No. Can we enjoy the intimacy of God's Spirit without entering into a covenant with Him? No. We have exhaustively studied how men and women become joined as one on earth, but how do we receive the Holy Spirit and become one with the Lord?

> **Read these verses and write down what a person did to be saved.**

Acts 2:37-47 _____

_____

Acts 8:9-13 _____

_____

Acts 8:26-40 _____

_____

Acts 9:17-18 _____

_____

Acts 10:42-48 _____

_____

Acts 16:11-15 _____

_____

Acts 16:25-34 _____

_____

Acts 18:5-8 _____

_____

Acts 19:1-7 _____

_____

Acts 22:11-16 _____

_____

Matthew 3:13-17 _____

_____

What should we say then? Should we continue in sin so that grace may multiply? Absolutely not! How can we who died to sin still live in it? Or are you unaware that all of us who were baptized into Christ Jesus were baptized into His death? Therefore we were buried with Him by baptism into death, in order that, just as Christ was raised from the dead by the glory of the Father, so we too may walk in a new way of life. For if we have been joined with Him in the likeness of His death, we will certainly also be in the likeness of His resurrection.

Romans 6:1-5 HCSB

You, however, are not in the flesh but in the Spirit, if in fact the Spirit of God dwells in you. Anyone who does not have the Spirit of Christ does not belong to him. But if Christ is in you, although the body is dead because of sin, the Spirit is life because of righteousness. If the Spirit of him who raised Jesus from the dead dwells in you, he who raised Christ Jesus from the dead will also give life to your mortal bodies through his Spirit who dwells in you.

Romans 8:9-11

11

THE CELEBRATION

young Hebrew bride's eyes would have always been on the horizon. Every day that passed meant that she was one day closer to hearing her husband call her name—claiming her as his own—and coming to take her home. However, two thousand years have passed since Jesus left His bride, and our eyes seem to have wandered.

But concerning that day and hour no one knows, not even the angels of heaven, nor the Son, but the Father only. For as were the days of Noah, so will be the coming of the Son of Man. For as in those days before the flood they were eating and drinking, marrying and giving in marriage, until the day when Noah entered the ark, and they were unaware until the flood came and swept them all away, so will be the coming of the Son of Man.

Matthew 24:36-39

> **Study 1 Corinthians 7:25-39. Does Paul's advice apply to us today? What do verses 29 and 31 indicate?**

_____

_____

_____

The hard truth we all must accept is that, most likely, we will die before we see Jesus. People die every day, yet death is the only unnatural part of our world. God designed His creation to be like Him: never-ending. God could have made us like animals, unaware of our personhood, but He left us living as a paradox: eternal beings trapped in a doomed existence. I imagine the early church was rocked by the martyrdom of Stephen and of the apostle James. They seemed to believe that Jesus was returning in their lifetimes. Paul writes to comfort the Christians in Thessalonica,

> We do not want you to be uninformed, brothers, concerning those who are asleep, so that you will not grieve like the rest, who have no hope. Since we believe that Jesus died and rose again, in the same way God will bring with Him those who have fallen asleep through Jesus. For we say this to you by a revelation from the Lord: We who are still alive at the Lord's coming will certainly have no advantage over those who have fall-

en asleep. For the Lord Himself will descend from heaven with a shout, with the archangel's voice, and with the trumpet of God, and the dead in Christ will rise first. Then we who are still alive will be caught up together with them in the clouds to meet the Lord in the air and so we will always be with the Lord. Therefore encourage one another with these words.

1 Thessalonians 4:13-18 HCSB

Take the time to read 1 Corinthians 15:35-58. Why would the Corinthians be curious as to how the dead are raised and what kind of body they will have? How should we view our death?

_____

_____

_____

Jesus spoke in parables often, yet also spoke quite plainly of events to come both near at hand and in the distant future.

Jesus left the temple and was going away, when his disciples came to point out to him the buildings of the temple. But he answered them, "You see all these, do you not? Truly, I say to you, there will not be left here one stone upon another that will not be thrown down." As he sat on the Mount of Olives, the disciples came to him privately, saying, "Tell us, when will these things be, and what will be the sign of your coming and of the end of the age?"

Matthew 24:1-3

The apostles asked two questions, and Jesus answered them. Read one of His answers in Matthew 24:4-14. What is Jesus speaking of? How are we to respond to tragedy in light of this prophecy?

_____

_____

_____

Read Matthew 24:15-28. How is this section different than the verses previously, and to what is it referring to? Find the Old Testament references in Daniel 11:31-35.

_____

_____

_____

Immediately after the tribulation of those days the sun will be darkened, and the moon will not give its light, and the stars will fall from heaven, and the powers of the heavens will be shaken. Then will appear in heaven the sign of the Son of Man, and then all the tribes of the earth will mourn, and they will see the Son of Man coming on the clouds of heaven with power and great glory. And he will send out his angels with a loud trumpet call, and they will gather his elect from the four winds, from one end of heaven to the other.

Matthew 24:29-31

The rest of chapter 24 and the entirety of 25 is dedicated to reiterating that Jesus will return when no one expects, and His followers have better be ready and doing the work Jesus has left for them. Read about the final judgment in Matthew 25:31-46.

Copy verse 34: _____
_____
_____
_____
_____

Jesus will then credit His Bride with many righteous acts that she had done for Him, but she is confused. This is the first time the Bride has met her Bridegroom. Jesus, however, responds, "Whatever you did for one of the least of these brothers of mine, you did for Me." By taking on flesh, Jesus became a brother of humanity. "He didn't have an impressive form or majesty that we should look at Him, no appearance that we should desire Him" (Isaiah 53:2b HCSB). Hospitality and charity were of utmost importance in Jewish culture. The Bride of Christ would be expected to serve all those around her out of the abundance gifted to her by her husband.

> Many struggle with the idea that God created mankind, which is inherently evil, only to punish us, but was that the plan at all according to Matthew 25:41 and Revelation 20:11-15?

The coming of Jesus will be the fulfillment of God's plan from day one: to live with His creation. A Jewish wedding celebration is seven days long, a sign of perfection and a nod to creation. Eternity with God will be different, however. Unlike Adam and Eve, we will know the cost and the worth of being able to dwell with God.

Read one of the most beautiful and comforting passages in the Bible, Revelation 21:1-11. The wife of the Lamb is described as a new Jerusalem. This city was set aside to be the dwelling place of God, the location on which the Temple was built. The new Jerusalem is illustrated as having unimaginably perfect and beautiful architecture: twelve gates made of pearls, twelve foundations, walls built of jasper, the city itself made of gold.

> What is the significance of the foundations of the new Jerusalem? Find the correlation between Revelation 21:14, 19-20 and Exodus 39:10-14.

———————————————————

———————————————————

We are, of course, this new Jerusalem. We are founded in the Law and Prophets of the Jews and brought to a full understanding of the Messiah through the Gospel. The detailed description of the city by John is a visual representation of who the Bride of Christ is and the richness of her heritage.

> And I saw no temple in the city, for its temple is the Lord God the Almighty and the Lamb. And the city has no need of sun or moon to shine on it, for the glory of God gives it light, and its lamp is the Lamb. By its light will the nations walk, and the kings of the earth will bring their glory into it, and its gates will never be shut by day—and there will be no night there. They will bring into it the glory and the honor of the nations.
>
> Revelation 21:22-26

Study Revelation 22. Do we have contact with this river before death? What is the significance of verse 14? How many times does Jesus say, "I am coming soon?"

———————————————————

———————————————————

———————————————————

The celebration of God is all that really matters. If our lives are not centered around being a part of this event, then we are lost and undeserving of God's amazing gift. God very clearly lays out how we enter His presence: by becoming the Bride of Christ.

THE BRIDE OF CHRIST

I am the vine, you are the branches. He who abides in Me, and I in him, bears much fruit; for without Me you can do nothing.

John 15:5 NKJV

Your wife will be like a fruitful vine within your house; your children will be like olive shoots around your table.

Psalm 128:3

Are you a part of the Bride of Christ? If you are not, Jesus is calling to you. He is pursuing you through His Word. He desperately wants to know you and be known by you more intimately and completely than any other relationship you have ever experienced.

As the Father has loved me, so have I loved you. Abide in my love. If you keep my commandments, you will abide in my love, just as I have kept my Father's commandments and abide in his love. These things I have spoken to you, that my joy may be in you, and that your joy may be full.

John 15:9-11

If you are ready to become a Bride of Christ, you can be washed in the blood of Jesus today. As the Ethiopian official said, "See, here is water! What prevents me from being baptized?" (Acts 8:36) Find a local group of believers, lean on the body of Christ, and dive into the Word of God.

If you are a part of the Bride of Christ and have neglected or even abandoned your relationship with Jesus, please know He has not stopped loving you. Like Hosea, He is waiting on you to return to Him. Things may be very difficult for you because He is hedging your way with thorns to keep you from pursing the idols you have set up in your life. He knows that when you are running away from Him you are running into the arms of pain, despair, and death. You were made for Jesus and He is made for you. Come back to Him.

> **Read Psalm 103 and dwell on God's love for you. How do you plan to change your relationship with God in light of how He feels about you?**

_____

_____

The final bride we will study is one of the most famous women in the Bible. She is universally identified as a hero, but I argue that the reason for her heroism is misplaced. Her story is extraordinary in its impact and scope, and yet still relatable to us today. This woman was born as Hadassah, but you probably know her as Esther.

> **Turn to Esther 2:8-11. Like Daniel, Shadrach, Meshach, and Abednego, Hadassah is put under government control while in exile, but what is the big difference between her and them?**

_____

_____

_____

When Esther steps into the king's bedchamber, fifty years and two kings have passed since the Jews were providentially allowed to return to their homeland, yet Esther and Mordecai remain. They heard the legends of their fellow Jews being saved from certain death and how the Lord wrote on the wall of the king's dining room pronouncing his imminent death, but they chose to stay in a foreign, pagan land. Mordecai had an enviable position among the royal staff at the king's gate and though his identity as a Jew was known, his name reflected the status of his loyalty. Mordecai literally means "servant of Marduk" who is the chief Babylonian deity, a god in the form of the cow, who is supposed to control the sun, battle, and fertility. When Mordecai advises his niece to hide her Jewish identity and change her name to Esther, which is derived from "Ishtar" the goddess of love and beauty, we can see where their priorities were.

However, "He has not dealt with us as our sins deserve or repaid us according to our offenses" (Psalm 103:10 HCSB). God blessed Esther and Mordecai even while they were unfaithful to Him. Esther becomes queen, Mordecai holds an important position in court, and for a while, God seems to be forgotten. However, an enemy, long in the making, surfaces forcing these wayward Jews to remember who they really are.

> **Read Esther 3:1-6. Why wouldn't Mordecai bow to Haman? Who were Mordecai and Haman's ancestors and how did this blood feud nearly change the course of history? Read Exodus 17:8-16, 1 Samuel 9:1-2, 1 Samuel 15:1-33, and Esther 2:5-6 to put the pieces together.**

While Mordecai was not dedicated to the God that brought him out of Egypt, he was ready to pick up a feud that went back hundreds of years, before even the reign of David. His racism was the spark that would have led to the systematic genocide of an entire race, had the Lord not intervened. Living apart from the Lord leads us to places we never imagined we would go and drags along the ones we love the most. Esther's obedience to her uncle led her to living a lie as the pagan queen of Persia. She would have worshiped their gods, ate their food, and worn amulets of their deities as signs of devotion. No one suspected that she was from the strange race that professed that there was only one God, who had no image that His people bowed down to and who required them to abstain from various foods and activities. Hadassah was part of a chosen people, a people that had made a covenant with the one true God, but she was ashamed of Him. God, however, does not forget His promises and never gives up on His bride.

> Seek the LORD while he may be found; call upon him while he is near; let the wicked forsake his way, and the unrighteous man his thoughts; let him return to the LORD, that he may have compassion on him, and to our God, for he will abundantly pardon. For my thoughts are not your thoughts, neither are your ways my ways, declares the LORD. For as the heavens are higher than the earth, so are my ways higher than your ways and my thoughts than your thoughts.
>
> Isaiah 55:6-9

God put Esther and Mordecai exactly where He needed them and worked His plan through their faults as well as their strengths, but ultimately, He needed their full obedience. Read Esther 4. What had to happen before Mordecai and Esther were willing to live as God's chosen people?

God uses broken people. God uses redeemed people. Only by giving up of ourselves of who we thought we wanted to be can God show us who we really are.

> For we are His workmanship, created in Christ Jesus for good works, which God prepared beforehand that we should walk in them.
> Ephesians 2:10 NKJV

> **According to the Jews, what are the intentions behind taking a bride? What is our main purpose as brides of Christ? Read Malachi 2:10-16.**

_____

_____

_____

We know that the reason for so many laws and customs surrounding marriage are to ensure that a man's wife produces a legitimate heir, an heir of his body that will bear his name. Likewise, we are called to be holy and set apart for the Lord because only then can we produce children of God.

> Therefore be imitators of God, as beloved children. And walk in love, as Christ loved us and gave himself up for us, a fragrant offering and sacrifice to God. But sexual immorality and all impurity or covetousness must not even be named among you, as is proper among saints. Let there be no filthiness nor foolish

talk nor crude joking, which are out of place, but instead let there be thanksgiving. For you may be sure of this, that everyone who is sexually immoral or impure, or who is covetous (that is, an idolater), has no inheritance in the kingdom of Christ and God.

Ephesians 5:1-5

If we are going to fulfill our purpose and produce spiritual children, then we must be holy and pure as a worthy bride should be.

I appeal to you therefore, brothers, by the mercies of God, to present your bodies as a living sacrifice, holy and acceptable to God, which is your spiritual worship. Do not be conformed to this world, but be transformed by the renewal of your mind, that by testing you may discern what is the will of God, what is good and acceptable and perfect.

Romans 12:1-2

We sing the silly song "Father Abraham" with our kids in Bible class, but have you ever considered yourself to be a "Daughter of Sarah?" Turn to 1 Peter 3:1-6 and list how we can emulate our spiritual matriarch.

The Spirit himself bears witness with our spirit that we are children of God, and if children, then heirs— heirs of God and fellow heirs with Christ, provided

we suffer with him in order that we may also be glo-
rified with him. For I consider that the sufferings of
this present time are not worth comparing with the
glory that is to be revealed to us.

Romans 8:16-18

Being a part of the Kingdom of God has no earthly glory or
prestige. Rather we are promised hard work and persecution. The
Bride of Christ is expected to pursue righteousness and perfection
(Matt. 5:48) while waiting for what was promised. Hebrews 11 lists
Abel, Enoch, Noah, Abraham, Jacob, Moses—so many who acted
in faith but did not receive what was promised them. They were
part of a grand plan that would reconcile God with humanity—
God with His Bride. These heroes of old labored and suffered so
that we could be part of the Kingdom of God. How can we not
work to be worthy of their sacrifice? How can we not find immea-
surable joy at being the center of so glorious a plan?

And all these, though commended through their
faith, did not receive what was promised, since God
had provided something better for us, that apart from
us they should not be made perfect. Therefore, since
we are surrounded by so great a cloud of witnesses, let
us also lay aside every weight, and sin which clings so
closely, and let us run with endurance the race that is
set before us, looking to Jesus, the founder and per-
fecter of our faith, who for the joy that was set before
him endured the cross, despising the shame, and is
seated at the right hand of the throne of God.

Hebrews 11:39-12:2

Every day brings us closer to Jesus. Every moment brings us closer to the fulfillment of God's awesome plan: to dwell with His bride for all eternity.

> And the Spirit and the bride say, "Come!" And let him who hears say, "Come!" And let him who thirsts come. Whoever desires, let him take the water of life freely.
>
> Revelation 22:17 NKJV